SRA Reading Mastery

Signature Edition

Storybook

Siegfried Engelmann
Elaine C. Bruner

SRA

Columbus, OH

SRAonline.com

 SRA

READING MASTERY ® is a registered trademark of The McGraw-Hill Companies, Inc.

The McGraw·Hill Companies

Table of Contents

I am lāt e. I āt e ham on a hill.

I āt e and āt e. and now I am

lāt e. I will run.

I wish I had sand. I wish I had a rāk_e. I wish I had a fish. I wish I had a lāk_e.

hē has a fat cat. hē has fun

with his fat cat.

his mom has a littlₑ cat. shē

has fun with thē littlₑ cat. thē

littlₑ cat has fun in thē sand.

a littlₑ fish sat on a fat fish.

thē littlₑ fish said, "wow."

thē littlₑ fish did not hāte thē

fat fish. thē littlₑ fish said,

"that fat fish is mom."

thē cow sat on a gāte. thē cow said, "thē gāte is hot." shē said, "I hāte hot gātes."

a fish āt_e a roc_k. thē fish

said, "I āt_e a roc_k."

a cow āt_e thē fish. thē cow

said, "I āt_e a fish. and now I

fēēl sic_k."

11

shē can kic_k. shē can lic_k. shē

said, "I am not a cat." shē said,

"I am not a fish."

is shē a man?

shē was not mad at him. did

shē hit him? nō, nō, nō. did shē

hug him? nō, nō, nō. did shē

kiss him?

hē said, "can I ēₐt a nut?"

shē said, "gō sit with thē

cow."

hē said, "nō. I will not gō."

shē said, "gō sit with thē cat."

hē said, "thē cat can ēₐt a nut."

shē said, "gō sit with thē cat

and ē.t."

sō hē āt. a nut. hē said, "this is

fun."

hē has nō fēēt. hē has nō

nōs_e. hē has nō tēēth. hē is not

a cow. and hē is not a cat.

is hē a rat? nō. hē is not a

rat.

I can kiss a cat. I can kiss

a kitt_en.

can a cow kiss mē? nō. a cow

can not kiss mē. a cow can

lic_k mē.

can a cat lic_k a kitt_en?

I hav_e a cow. thē cow is fat.

I hav_e a cat. thē cat is fat.

how can I tāk_e thē cow and

thē cat with mē? can thē cow

sit on thē cat? nō.

wē havₑ hats. I can hōld thē

hats. thē cow can hōld thē hats.

an ōld man can hōld thē hats.

can a fat rat hōld thē hats?

wē sāv₍ₑ₎ roc₍ₖ₎s. wē sāv₍ₑ₎ sac₍ₖ₎s

and sac₍ₖ₎s of roc₍ₖ₎s. wē sāv₍ₑ₎

lots and lots of roc₍ₖ₎s.

wē hav₍ₑ₎ lots of littl₍ₑ₎ roc₍ₖ₎s.

wē sit on roc₍ₖ₎s. and wē giv₍ₑ₎

an ōld man lots of roc₍ₖ₎s.

thē ōld man said, "I can

shāve a cat." sō hē did.

thē ōld man said, "I can shāve

a cow." sō hē did.

thē ōld man said, "I can shāve

a rock."

did hē shāv_e a roc_k? nō.

hē said, "givₑ mē a hat ōr a

soc ₖ." sō shē gāvₑ him a soc ₖ

fōr his nōsₑ.

hē said, "I nēēd socₖs on thē

fēēt, not on thē nōsₑ." sō shē

gāvₑ him socₖs fōr his fēēt.

thē ōld man was cōld. hē did

not havₑ a hat ōr a cō͞at ōr socₖs.

sō hē got a gō͞at with lots of

hats and cō͞ats and socₖs.

now thē ōld man is not cōld

and thē gō͞at is not cōld.

the ōld gōₐt had an ōld cōₐt.

the ōld gōₐt said, "I will ēₐt this

ōld cōₐt." sō shē did.

"that was fun," shē said. "I ātₑ

the ōld cōₐt. and now I am cōld."

now the ōld gōₐt is sad.

the fat man and his fat cow

got on a littl_e roc_k.

a cat said, "fat man, that roc_k

will not hōld a fat man and his

co... ...hat roc_k will gō down

thē hill."

did thē roc_k gō down thē hill

with thē fat man and his fat

cow?

thē rat had fun. hē ran in

thē sand.

hē had sand on his fēēt. hē

had sand on his ēars. hē had

sand on his nōse. hē had sand

on his tāil.

hē said, "I havₑ a lot of sand

on mē."

shē said, "I haVe a fan."

hē said, "I haVe sand."

shē said, "wē can run thē

sand in thē fan." sō hē ran thē

fan nēar thē sand.

hē had sand in his ēars. hē

said, "I can not hēar."

hē had sand on his sēat. shē

said, "wē havₑ sand on us."

a dog sat in a littlₑ car. thē

dog said, "I nēēd to ēat."

will thē dog ēat a fish? nō.

will thē dog ēat a log? nō. will

thē dog ēat a pot of tar? nō.

thē dog will ēat thē car.

a dog was in thē fog. a cat

was in thē fog. a gōat was in

thē fog.

thē dog and thē cat and thē

gōat cāme to a log.

thē cat and thē dog sat on thē

log. thē dog and thē cat said,

"wē arₑ on thē log."

thē gōat said, "I am not on

thē log. I am in thē log. ha ha."

thē fat man and his dog had

a car. thē car did not run.

sō thē fat man and his dog

got a gōat. thē fat man and

his dog sat on thē gōat. thē gōat

did not gō.

thē fat man said, "thē gō̯at

will not gō."

sō thē fat man and his dog

sat on thē rō̯ad.

lots of cars

a man on a farm has lots of

cars. hē has ōld cars. hē has

littlₑ cars.

arₑ his cars fōr gōats? nō.

are his cars fōr shēēp? nō. are

his cars fōr cows? nō.

his cars are fōr cops. hē has

lots of cop cars.

thē girl and thē dog

thē girl said, "I can tēₐch thē

dog to run."

thē dog said, "nō."

thē girl said, "I will tēₐch thē

dog to run."

thē dog said, "nō. thē girl can

not tēₐch mē to run. I can run.

ha ha."

a girl in a cāv_e

a girl was in a cāv_e. a wāv_e

cām_e in thē cāv_e. thē girl said,

"sāv_e mē, sāv_e mē."

a fish cām_e in thē cāv_e. shē

said, "I will sāve that girl."

and shē did.

the fish said, "now I will give

that girl a sēēd and a ham to

ēat." sō shē gāve thē girl a sēēd

and a ham.

lots of pots

a girl said, "that man has lots of pots. hē has pots with tops. hē has pots with nō tops."

the man said, "I havₑ lots of cākₑs in pots. I havₑ a pot with a ship in it. I havₑ fish in pots."

the girl said, "can I have a pot for

a little fish?"

the man said, "this is a pot for a

little fish."

the girl said, "I will take this pot

home with me." and she did.

al and sal

al said, "will wē gō hōme?"

sal said, "nō. wē will gō to that farm."

al said, "will wē have fun on that

farm?"

sal said, "wē can run with a cow.

wē can ēat cōrn. wē can fēēd pigs. wē

can sit in the lāke."

al said, "I hāte to sit in lākes."

sō sal and al did not sit in the lāke.

sal and al had fun with the pigs.

a fish in the rāin

ron met pat in the rāin. ron got wet.

pat got wet.

ron said, "this is not fun."

pat said, "this is fun."

ron said, "I hav‌e wet fēēt. sō I

will gō hōm‌e. I do not nēēd rāin."

pat said, "wē can get fish."

sō shē got a fish and gāve it to him.

ron said, "it is fun to get wet if wē

get fish."

the pet shop

a girl said to a man, "let us gō to the pet shop." sō the man and the girl went down the rōad.

the man and the girl went in the pet shop. the girl said to the man in the pet shop, "I nēēd a dog."

the man said, "nō. I do not haνe dogs.

I haνe a red cat. let mē get that cat."

sō hē did. and the girl went hōme with

the red cat.

the cow on the rōad

lots of men went in a littl**e** car. the

men went down a rōad.

a cow sat on the rōad. the cow did

not get up. sō the men ran to the cow.

the men said, "wē will lift this cow."

the men did not lift the cow. "this cow

is sō fat wē can not lift it."

the cow said, "I am not sō fat. I can

lift mē." the cow went in the car.

the men said, "now wē can not get

in the car." sō the men sat on the rōad

and the cow went hōme in the car.

a girl and a gōat

a girl was on the rōad to a farm. shē

met a gōat. shē said, "gō with mē to the

farm. wē will pet a pig."

the gōat said, "I pet ducks and I

pet chicks. I do not pet pigs."

the girl said, "it is fun to pet pigs.

pigs ar_e fat."

the gōa_t said, "I will not gō to the farm. I will gō to the park and pet a ducк."

sō the gōa_t went to the park to pet a ducк. and the girl went to the farm to pet a pig.

pāᵢnt that nōsₑ

a fat dog met a littlₑ dog. the fat dog

had a red nōsₑ. the littlₑ dog had a red

nōsₑ.

the fat dog said, "I havₑ a red nōsₑ."

the littlₑ dog said, "I wish I did not

havₑ a red nōsₑ."

the fat dog got a can of pāint. hē
said, "pāint that nōse."

sō the little dog did pāint his nōse. hē
said, "now this nōse is not red."

hē kissed the fat dog on the ēar. now
the fat dog has pāint on his ēar.

the red hat

the fish had a car and nō hat. shē

said, "I do not nēēd a car. I nēēd a

red hat."

shē met a cow. the cow had a red hat.

the fish said, "can I have that red hat?"

the cow said, "nō."

the fish said, "I will giv_e that cow a

car if sh_ē will let m_ē hav_e the hat."

the cow said, "t_āk_e the hat and giv_e

m_ē a car." s_ō the fish got a red hat

and the cow got a car.

a bug and a dog

a bug and a dog sat on a log. the

dog said, "that bug is sō littlₑ I can not

sēē him on the log."

the bug said, "I am big."

the dog said, "that bug on the log

is not big."

the bug said, "I will ēₐt this log."

and hē did. hē bit and bit and bit at the

log. the bug said, "now that dog can sēē

how big I am."

the dog said, "that bug can ēₐt logs

as well as a big bug can."

the bugs →

a big bug met a little bug. the big bug

said, "let's gō ēat." sō the big bug āte a

lēaf and a nut and a rock. the big bug

said, "that is how big bugs ēat."

the little bug said, "now I will ēat."

sō the little bug āte a lēaf and a nut and

a roc_k. then the littl_e bug went to a log

and bit the log. shē āt_e the log. then shē

āt_e ten mōr_e logs.

"wow," the big bug said. "that littl_e

bug can ēat a lot."

the littl_e bug said, "now let's ēat mōr_e."

the bug bus

a little bug sat on the back of a big
dog. "get down," said the dog. "I am not
a bus."

the bug did not get down. shē went to
slēēp. the dog said, "I am not a bed."

the dog ran to the pond and went in.

the bug got wet. the bug said, "I am not a fish. tāke mē back to the sand."

"nō," the dog said.

sō the bug said, "I will get mōre bugs on this dog." ten bugs cāme and got on the dog.

the dog said, "I fēēl lIke a bug bus."

and the dog went back to the sand with

the bugs.

the man and his bed

a man had a tub. hē said, "I līke to

sit in the tub and rub, rub, rub."

then the man said, "now I will slēēp in

this bed." but a dog was in his bed.

the dog said, "can I slēēp in this bed?"

the man said, "nō. gō slēēp in the tub."

the dog said, "I līke to slēēp in beds."

the man said, "this dog līkes to slēēp

in beds. sō hē can slēēp with mē. but I

do not līke dogs that bīte."

the dog said, "I do not līke to bīte."

sō the man and the dog went to slēēp.

and the dog did not bīte the man.

the talking cat

the girl was going for a walk. she met

a fat cat. "can cats talk?" the girl said.

the cat said, "I can talk. but I do not

talk to girls. I talk to dogs."

the girl did not like that cat. "I do

not like cats that will not talk to me."

the cat said, "I will not talk to girls."

the girl said, "I do not līke that cat.

and I do not give fish to cats I do not

līke."

the cat said, "I līke fish sō I will

talk to this girl." sō the girl and the cat

āte fish.

the dog that āte fish

a girl went fishing with a dog. that

dog āte fish. the girl did not līke the

dog to ēat fish. "do not ēat the fish," shē

said.

the girl went fishing and the dog went

to slēēp. the girl got fīve fish.

"give me the five fish," the dog said.

"no," the girl said. "more fish are in the lake. dive in and get them."

so the dog went in the lake. and the girl went to sleep.

the end

the rat got a sōre nōse

a rat and a rabbit went down a slīde.

the rabbit went down on his tāil. the

rat said, "I will gō down on the tāil."

the rat went up to the top of the slīde

and slid down on his nōse. hē said, "I

have a sōre nōse."

then hē said, "if a rabbit can gō down

on his tāil, I will do the sāme." hē went

up to the top. but hē cāme down on his

nōse.

the rabbit said, "that rat can not tell

if hē is on his nōse ōr his tāil."

the end

the rich pig

a dog was in the park. it was dark in

the park.

shē ran into a pig. shē said,

"pigs can not gō in this park. pigs live

on farms."

the pig said, "not this pig. I live on a

ship. I am a rich pig."

the dog said, "tāke mē to the ship."

sō the pig did.

but the wāves māde the ship rock.

and the dog got sick.

the end

digging in the yard

a little man had a fat dog. the dog

lived in the yard. the dog dug a hōle in

the yard. the little man got mad. "dogs

can not dig in this yard. I will gō fōr a

cop." the dog dug and dug.

the man got a cop. the man said, "that

dog dug a big hōle in the yard."

the cop said, "dogs can not dig in

this yard."

the dog said, "I will stop. can I bē

a cop dog?"

the cop said, "yes. I nēēd a cop dog."

the end

ron said, "yes"

ron's dad tōld him to slēēp in bed.

"yes," ron said. and hē did.

his mom said, "ron, pāint this bed

red."

"yes," ron said. hē got the pāint and

māde the bed red.

"that is fīne," his mom said.

a big bōy met ron. hē said, "can ron

pāint a car red?"

"yes," ron said. and hē māde the car

red.

then ron went hōme. his mom said,

"ron māde a bed red and a car red. but

ron got lots of paint on ron. ron is red."

sō ron went to the tub and went rub,

rub, rub. now ron is not red.

this is the end.

gōing to the park

a bōy met fīve girls. hē said, "let's gō to the park."

a girl said, "wē can not sēē the park. is the park nēar hēre?"

the bōy said, "nō. wē nēēd a car to get to the park."

the girls said, "wē do not hаvе a car."

the bōy said, "wē can not walk to the

park. and wē can not rīdе to the park.

how will wē get to the park?"

the girls said, "let's run." sō the bōy

and the girls ran to the park.

this is the end.

hunting fōr a dēer

ann said to her dad, "let's gō fīnd a dēer fōr a pet."

sō ann and her dad went hunting fōr a dēer. a dēer cāme up to them. ann said, "you can bē a pet."

the dēer said, "nō, a dēer is not a pet.

dogs ar_e pets. and cats ar_e pets. I am
not a pet. but I will let a girl and her
dad pet mē."

the girl said, "that will bē fun." it was.
now, the girl has a pet dog and a pet
cat. they gō with her to hunt fōr the
dēēr that shē can pet.

the end

a card fōr mother

a bōy sent a card to his mother. the card said, "mother, I love you." but his mother did not get the card.

a cop got the card. shē said, "I am not mother." sō shē gāve the card to her brother.

her brother said, "this card is not

fōr mē. I am not mother."

sō the cop and her brother went to

fīnd mother. they met the bōy.

the bōy said, "you havₑ the card that

I sent to mother. givₑ mē that card."

sō they gāvₑ him the card.

and hē gāve the card to his mother.

this is the end.

the duck and the mēan pig

a mother duck and her nīne little ducks went fōr a walk. a big mēan pig met them on the rōad. shē tōld the mother duck, "I am a mēan pig. I ēat cans and I ēat bēans. I ēat cars and I ēat tōys. I ēat beds and I ēat bugs."

the mother duck said, "I am not a can ōr a bēan ōr a car ōr a tōy. I am a duck. and I bīte pigs that ar_e mē_an."

sō the pig ran. then the mother duck and her

nīn_e little ducks went to the pond.

the end

gōing to the tōy shop

a bōy and his mother went to a tōy shop. they went to get tōys. the bōy said, "I līke tōys. I līke big tōys."

his mother said, "I do not līke big tōys. sō wē will get little tōys."

the man in the tōy shop said, "wē have a lot of tōys. wē have tōys fōr bōys. wē have tōys fōr girls.

and wē havₑ tōys fōr dogs."

the bōy said, "I am not a dog. I am a bōy. and I līkₑ big tōys."

stop

going to the toy shop

a boy and his mother went shopping for toys.

the boy liked big toys. but his mother liked little toys.

the man in the toy shop said, "I have toys that you will like. they are big and little."

the boy said, "toys can not be big and little."

the man said, "these toys are big and little."

hē got a little tōy duck and hē māde it big. →

this is the end. →

the fat fox and his brother

a fat fox and his brother went into a big box.

the fat fox said, "I hāte to sit in a box."

his brother said, "sittiñg in a box is not a lot of

fun. let's hit the box. I love to hit a box."

the fat fox said, "I will hit the box with this

hand and this nōse and this tāil." sō hē hit and hit.

then the fat fox said, "it is gettiñg hot in this

box. let's stop hitting."

his brother said, "let's gō to slēēp. slēēping in a

box is fun." sō they went to slēēp.

this is the end.

the other sīde of the lāke

a bug sat on the shōre of a big lāke. the bug said, "I nēēd to get to the other sīde of this big lāke."

but the bug did not līke to get wet. hē said, "I līke to slēēp and I līke to rīde in a car. but I do not līke to get wet."

the bug did not have a car and hē did not have

a bed. sō hē sat and sat on the shōre of the lāke.

stop

the other sīde of the lāke

a bug sat and sat on the shōre of a lāke. hē did
not have a car to tāke him to the other sīde.

then a big ēagle cāme and sat down on the shōre.
the ēagle said, "you are sitting on the shōre and
you are sad."

the bug said, "yes. I am sad. I nēēd to get to
the other sīde of the lāke. I will give you a dīme."

the ēagle said, "yes. givе mē a dīmе and I will tākе you to the other sīdе." sō the bug gāvе the ēagle a dīmе and got on the ēagle. they went ōver the lākе.

the end

the pig that bit his leg

a little bug and a pig met on the rōₐd. the pig said, "I can walk better than you."

the little bug said, "but I can ēat better than you." then shē bit a log.

the pig said, "I can ēat logs better than you."

the pig went bīte, bīte, bīte and āte the log.

the bug said, "I can bīte a pig better than you."

shē bit the pig on the leg.

the pig said, "I can do better than that." the pig

gāve his leg a big bīte.

the bug said, "you bīte pigs better than mē."

the end

the cat that talk_ed

a girl had a little cat. shē loved her cat. shē went to the shop with her cat. shē went to the park with her cat. shē loved her cat.

the other dāy, shē was sittiñg with her cat in the park. shē said, "I love you, little cat. you ar_e never bad. you ar_e fun. but you can not talk to mē and that mākes mē sad."

the cat said, "I can talk to you."

stop

the cat that talked

a girl had a cat. shē loved her cat. shē talked to her cat.

then the cat talked to her. the girl said, "I must bē sleeping. cats can not talk."

the cat said, "you talk to mē. sō I can talk to you."

the girl gāve the cat a big hug. "I never had a

cat that talkₑd."

the cat said, "I never had a cat that talkₑd

ēithₑr." the girl and the cat talkₑd and talkₑd.

then ann cāmₑ to the park. shē went up to the

girl and said, "can I havₑ that cat?"

the cat said, "I will not gō with you."

ann said, "I must bē slēēpiñg. cats do not talk. I

will lēₐvₑ this park." and shē did.

the end

finding some fun on the moon

some girls went to the moon in a moon ship.

a girl said, "I will find some fun." she walked

and walked. soon she came to a cow.

the moon cow said, "we have lots of fun. come

with me." the girl went with the moon cow to a

pool. the moon cow said, "this is how we have fun

on the moon." she jumped into the pool. and the

girl jumped into the pool.

the girl said, "it is fun to swim on the moon." so
the girl and the cow went swimming every day. the
girl did not tell the other girls that she went
swimming with a moon cow.

the end

will the ōld car start?

a man had an ōld car. the ōld car did not start.

sō the man went down the rōad. soon hē cāme to a

rat.

the man said, "can you start an ōld car?"

the rat said, "nō. rats do not have cars."

sō the man went down the rōad. soon hē cāme to

a big man. hē said, "can you start an ōld car?"

the big man said, "yes. I can but I will not. I
am sitting. I never start cars if I am sitting."

the man said, "you can sit in the car if you can
start it."

so the big man got in the car and māde the car
start. hē said, "I līke this ōld car. sō I will kēēp
sitting in it." and hē did.

the end

the ōld man fīnds a hōrse

an ōld hōrse was in a barn. hē said, "I am sad.

I can not fīnd a man that will rīde on mē." hē

said to the cat, "have you sēēn a man that will rīde

on mē?"

the cat said, "nō."

an ōld man was walking nēar the barn. hē said to

the cat, "I can not fīnd a hōrse to rīde. have you

sēēn a hōrs_e that I can rīd_e?"

the cat said, "yes. hē is in the barn."

then the ōld man walk_ed into the barn. hē went up to the ōld hōrs_e. the ōld man said, "ōld hōrs_e, do you līk_e to gō fōr a rīd_e?"

the ōld hōrs_e said, "yes." sō the ōld man and the ōld hōrs_e went rīding.

the end

rēₐd the Ītem →

I. if the tēₐcher says "gō," stand up. →

bill went fishīng →

bill lĪkₑd to gō fishīng but hē did not get fish. the →
other bōys went fishīng and got lots of fish. a big →
bōy got fĪvₑ fish. a little bōy got nĪnₑ fish. but →
bill did not get fish. →

bill was mad. hē said, "I wish I had fish lĪkₑ the →

other boys." but nō fish cāme to his līne.

then hē had a tug on his līne. "I have a fish," hē said. but it was not a fish. it was an ōld box.

stop

rēₐd the Ītem ➤

1. if the tēₐcher says "now," hōld up your hand. ➤

bill went fishing ➤

bill went fishing with the other bōys. but hē did ➤
not get fīve fish. hē did not get nīne fish. hē got ➤
an ōld box. ➤

the other bōys māde fun of bill. "wē have fish ➤
and you do not. you have an ōld box." ➤

bill was sad. hē hit the box. the top fell down. and

bill said, "that box is filled with gōld."

bill was not sad. hē said to the other bōys, "you

have lots of fish, but I have lots of gōld."

this is the end.

rēₐd the Ītem

I. if the tēₐcher says "now," hōld up your hands.

an ōld hōrsₑ and an ēₐglₑ

an ōld hōrsₑ and an ēₐglₑ sat on a hill. the ēₐglₑ said, "it is fun to flȳ. mȳ mother līkₑs to flȳ. mȳ brother līkₑs to flȳ. and I līkₑ to flȳ."

the ōld hōrsₑ said, "can you tēₐch mē how to flȳ?"

the ēₐgle said, "I will flȳ to the top of the

barn." and hē did.

the ōld hōrse said, "I will flȳ to the top of the

barn." sō hē ran down the hill. and hē ran into the

sīde of the barn. hē said, "you did not tēₐch mē

how to flȳ."

stop

rēₐd the Ītem

1. when the tēₐcher says "do it," pick up your book.

an ōld hōrsₑ and an ēₐgle

an ēₐgle was tēₐchiñg an ōld hōrsₑ how to flȳ.

but the ōld hōrsₑ did not flȳ. the ōld hōrsₑ ran into

the sĪdₑ of a barn.

the ēₐgle said, "I will flȳ to the top of the car."

and hē did.

but the ōld hōrse did not flȳ to the top of the

car. hē ran into the sīde of the car. hē said, "mȳ

mother and mȳ brother can not flȳ. I can not flȳ."

the ēagle said, "if you can not flȳ, you can not

have fun."

the hōrse said, "I can run with an ēagle on mȳ

back, and that is fun."

sō the ēagle sat on the back of the ōld hōrse and

the ōld hōrse ran. "yes, this is fun," they said.

the end

rēₐd the Ītems

1. when the tēₐcher says "gō," pat your ēars.

2. when the tēₐcher says "do it," touch your fēēt.

the red tooth brush

a girl had a red tooth brush. shē lĪkₑd her red

tooth brush. shē brushₑd her tēēth six tĪmₑs a dāy.

shē said, "mȳ tēēth arₑ whĪtₑ. they arₑ sō whĪtₑ

they shĪnₑ lĪkₑ the moon."

the girl had a dog, but his tēēth did not shīne.

the girl went to brush her tēēth. but shē did not sēē her tooth brush. "I do not sēē mȳ red tooth brush," shē said.

shē went to her mother. "I nēēd mȳ red tooth brush."

but her mother said, "I do not have your red tooth brush."

stop

rēₐd the Ītems

1. when the tēₐcher says "stand up," pick up your

book.

2. if the tēₐcher says "now," hōld up your hands.

the red tooth brush

a girl lĪked to brush her tēēth. shē looked fōr

her red tooth brush. but her mother did not have it.

the girl went back to her room. on the wāy, shē

slipped and fell. shē slipped on her dog. her dog

was brushing his tēēth with her red tooth brush.

the girl said, "you have mȳ red tooth brush."

the dog said, "I līke tēēth that shīne līke the

moon."

the girl smīled and the dog smīled. they said,

"now wē bōth have tēēth that shīne līke the moon."

the end

rēₐd the Ītems ➤

1. if the tēₐcher stands up, touch your hand. ➤

2. if the tēₐcher says "stand up," touch your nōsₑ. ➤

the fat ēₐglₑ ➤

an ēₐglₑ lĪkₑd to ēat. hē ātₑ cākₑ and ham and ➤

cōrn. hē ātₑ and ātₑ, and hē got fatter and fatter. ➤

hē said, "I am sō fat that I can not flȳ." ➤

hē sat in a trēē and the other ēₐglₑs mādₑ fun of ➤

him. they said, "look at that fat, fat ēagle. hō, hō."

but then a tīger cāme hunting fōr ēagles. a little

ēagle sat under a trēē. the tīger went after the

little ēagle. the other ēagles yelled and yelled, but the

little ēagle did not hēar them.

stop

rēₐd the Ītems

1. when the tēₐcher says "touch your fēēt," stand

up.

2. if the tēₐcher says "gō," touch your ēₐrs.

the fat ēₐgle

a fat, fat ēₐgle was sitting in a trēē when a tĪger

cāme hunting fōr ēₐgles. the tĪger went after a

little ēₐgle that was sitting under the trēē. the other

ēagles yelled, but the little ēagle did not hēar them.

the fat, fat ēagle looked down and said, "I must sāve the little ēagle." sō hē jumped from the trēē. hē cāme down līke a fat rock on the tīger. and the tīger ran far awāy.

now the other ēagles do not māke fun of the fat, fat ēagle. they give him cāke and ham and cōrn.

this is the end.

rēad the Ītems

1. if the tēₐcher says "touch your nōsₑ," touch your fēēt.

2. when the tēₐcher says "givₑ mē your book," givₑ the tēₐcher your book.

a man līked to gō fast

a man līked to gō fast. hē went fast in his car. hē walked fast and hē ran fast. hē ēven talked fast. his wīfe did not līke him to gō sō fast. but hē went fast.

hē sat down to ēat an egg and a fish cāke and a mēat pīe. but hē āte sō fast that the egg slipped and fell on his fēēt.

hē bent down fast and his nōse went into the

fish cāke. hē went to wīpe his nōse fast and hē hit

the mēat pīe. the mēat pīe hit his wīfe.

stop

rēₐd the Ītems

1. when the tēₐcher says "touch your heₐd," hōld up

your hands.

2. if the tēₐcher picks up a book, sāy "now."

a man līkₑd to gō fast

a man did things fast. hē went fast in his

car. hē walkₑd fast. hē talkₑd fast. hē ēven ātₑ fast.

and when hē ātₑ, hē got egg on his fēēt and fish cākₑ

on his nōse.

the man said, "I will slōw down. I will not do things fast."

sō the man did not gō fast in his car. hē did not walk fast. hē did not talk fast. and hē did not ēat sō fast that hē got fish cāke on his nōse.

this is the end.